Counting Dragonflies

Counting Book For Toddlers
Coloring Book Included

Brenda J. Sullivan
Kathryn A. Sullivan

Counting Dragonflies

ISBN: 978-1-7329990-3-9

Published by Tree Roots Press

Photography
Brenda J. Sullivan
Artwork
Brenda J. Sullivan
Kathryn A. Sullivan
Google Images - Creative Commons License
Wikipedia

Requests to publish work from this book should be sent to:
Treerootspress@gmail.com
brenda@brendajsullivanbooks.com

Tree Roots Press

treerootspress.com

Dedicated to those who believe in the magic of dragonflies!

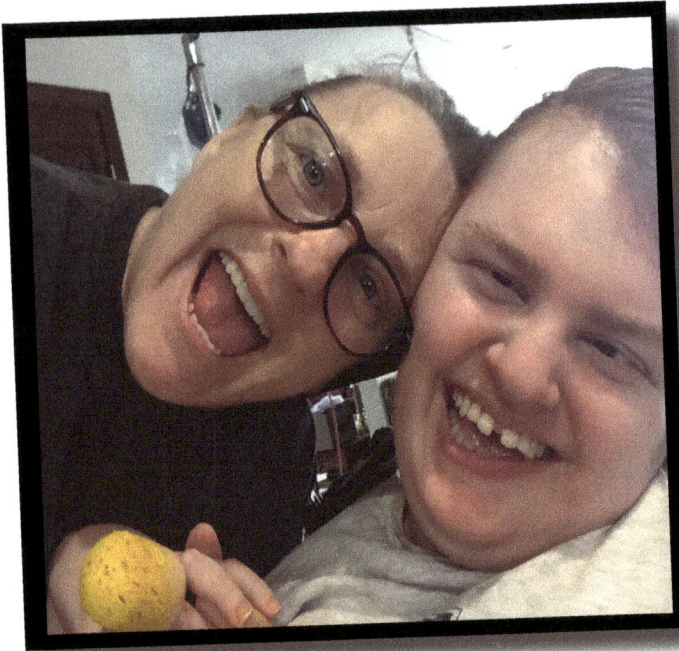

Katie with Mommy being silly while we paint

Katie with Daddy on one of our beach walks

This is how all our paintings start out.

Meet the Artist!

Katie

Katie is a wheelchair-bound young lady with severe cerebral palsy and epilepsy among many other medical problems. She is also nonverbal with very limited vision. Despite these challenges, she has a fighting spirit and has learned how to use basic communication skills and assistive technology to produce various arts and craft products.

This is one of Katie's "Able Gifts" – a product she's helped create with her Mother, Brenda J. Sullivan, when she is in good health and "able" to do so. Proceeds from these books are used to support the costs of Katie's craft-works and enable her to more fully engage her world.

Katie is excited when a whale swims by the window at the sea aquarium

1

One Dragonfly

2

Two Dragonflies

3

Three Dragonflies

4

Four Dragonflies

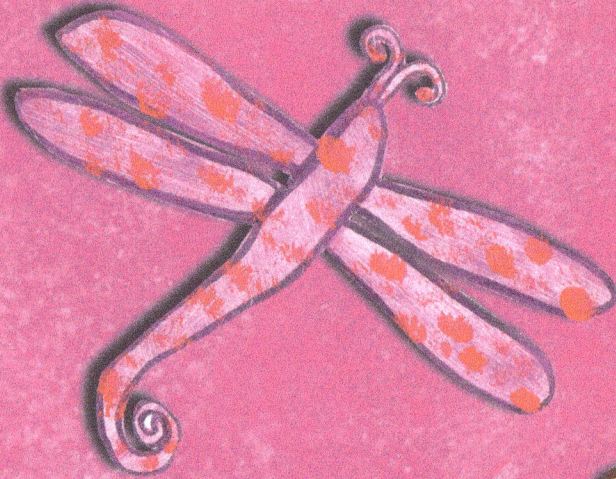

5

Five Dragonflies

6

Six Dragonflies

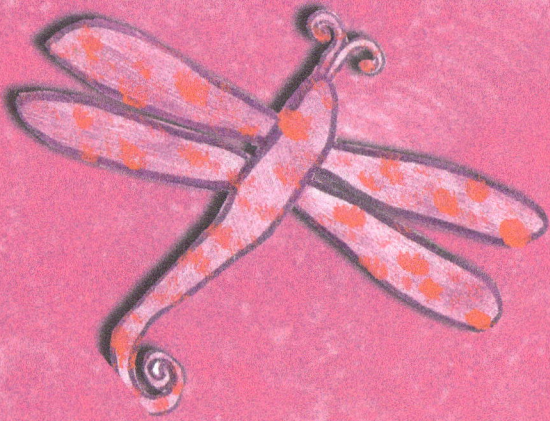

7

Seven Dragonflies

8

Eight Dragonflies

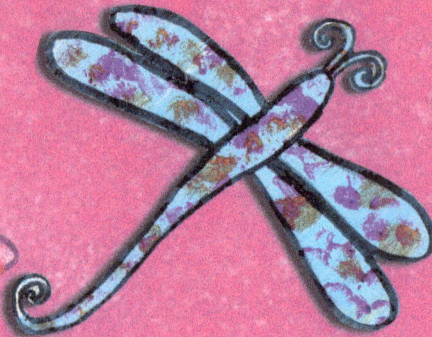

9

Nine Dragonflies

10

Ten Dragonflies

Dragonflies are expert fliers. They can fly straight up, down, hover like a helicopter or steal a kiss from their mate without landing.

This is a Globe Skimmer Dragonfly that lives primarily in the tropics but is also found in North America and Europe.

It can travel over 11,000 miles while migrating back and forth following warm weather.

This is a fossil of a dragonfly that scientists believe were some of the first winged insects to evolve over 300 million years ago.

Fun Facts About Dragonflies

- There are more than 5000 species of dragonflies in the world.

- Dragonflies eat their prey while flying, and if unable to fly, they will starve to death.

- Most often, dragonflies catch their prey with their feet.

- A dragonfly's eye is so big that it's really its head.

- Dragonflies live on every continent except Antarctica. It's too cold for them to survive in that frozen climate, and dragonflies prefer warmer temperatures like the tropics.

- Dragonflies live in areas where it's moist, wet or where there are pools of water. Places like rainforests, wetlands, forests, streams, ponds, and lakes.

- In many parts of the world, development has destroyed their habitat or home. If this continues, many species of dragonflies are in danger of becoming extinct.

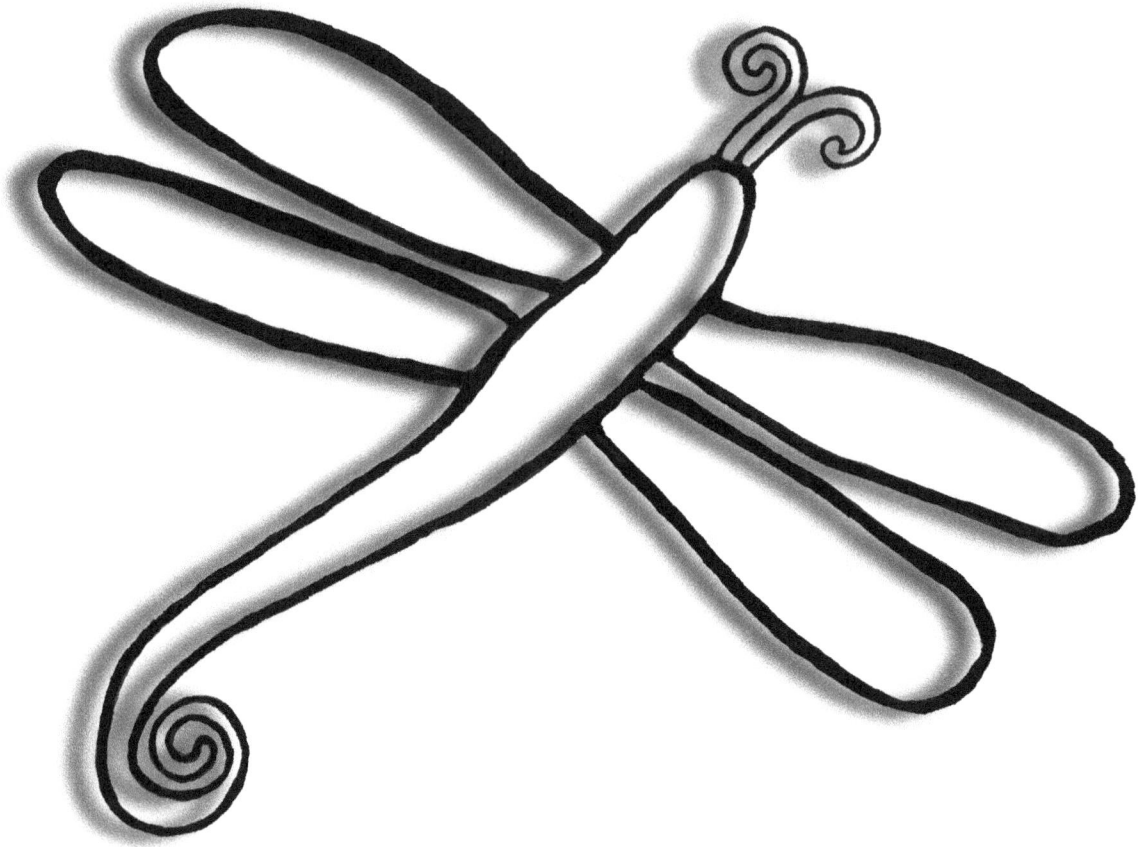

1

One Dragonfly

2

Two Dragonflies

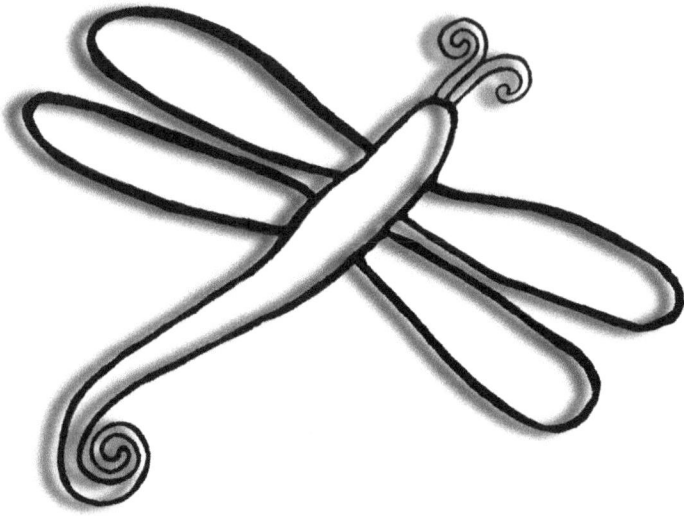

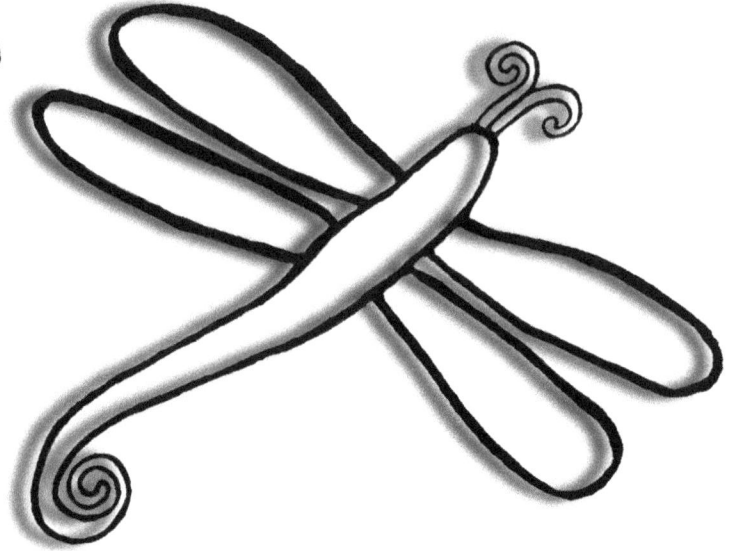

3

Three Dragonflies

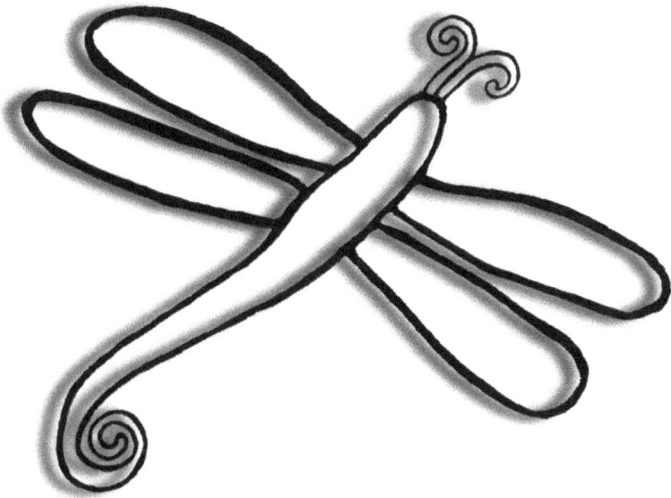

4

Four Dragonflies

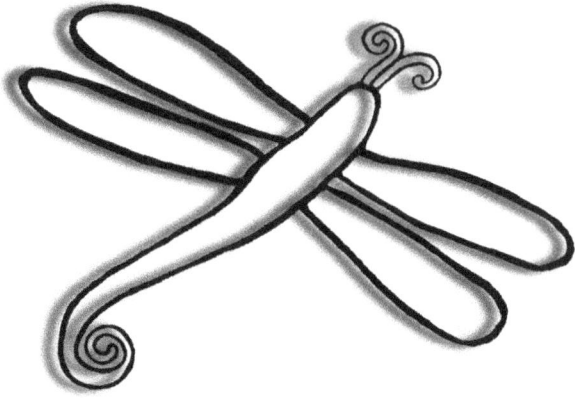

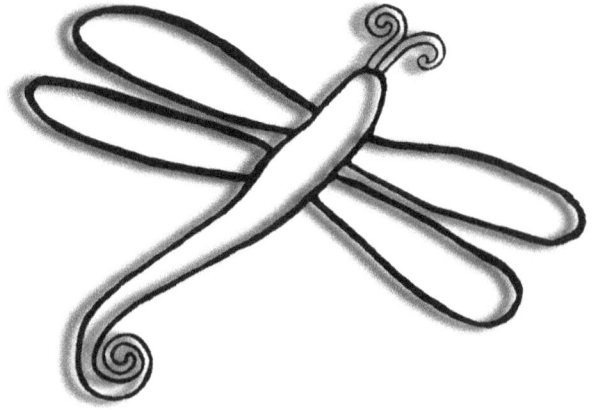

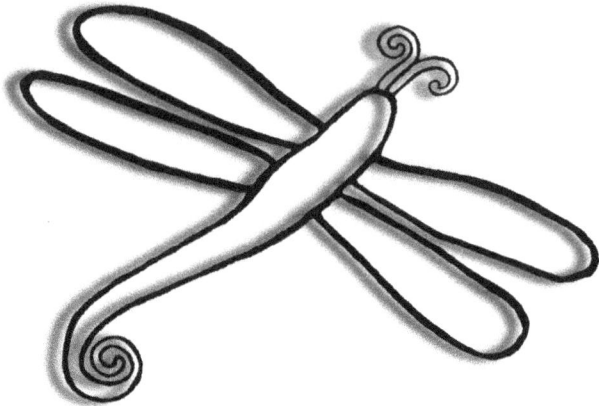

5

Five Dragonflies

6

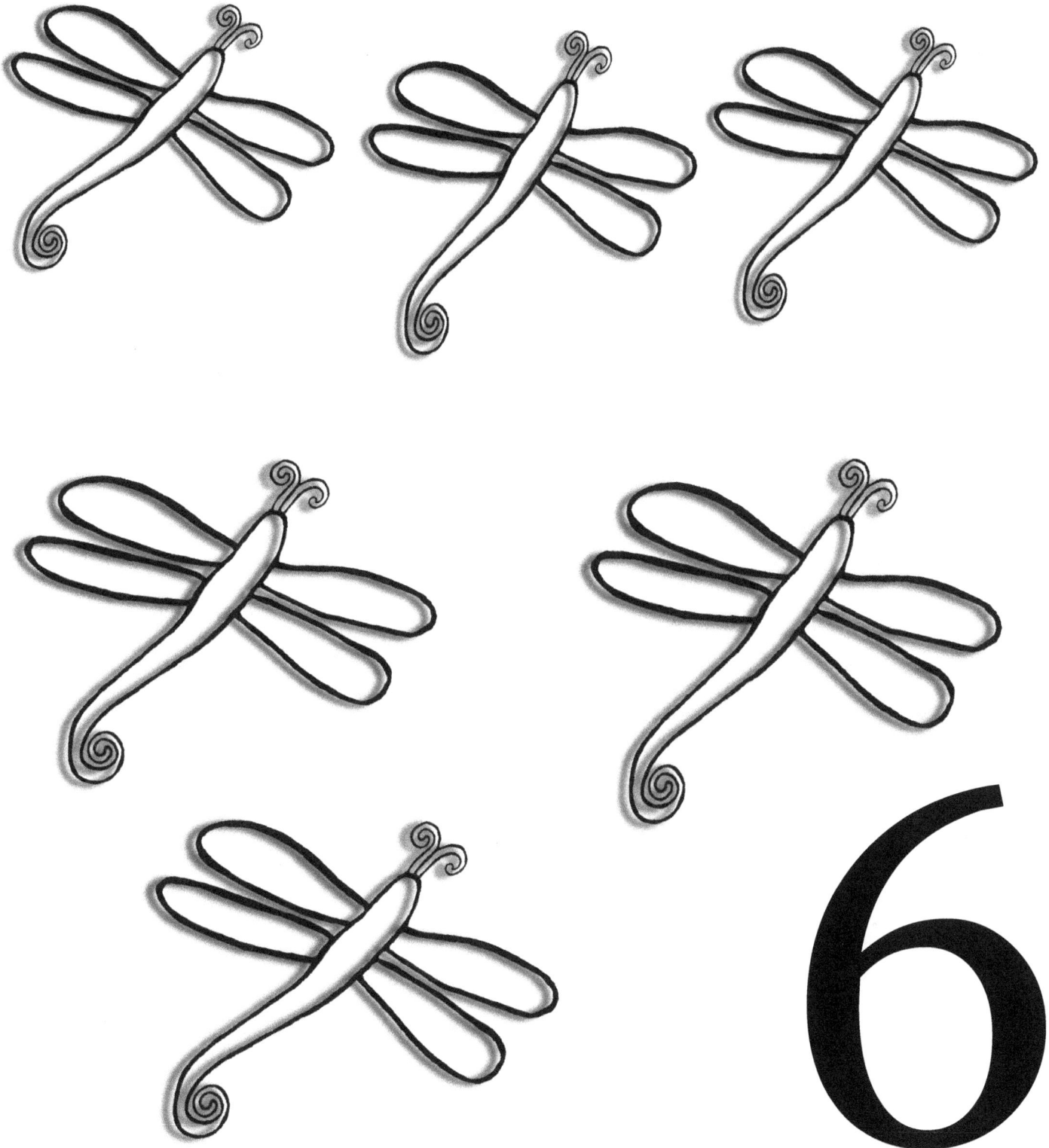

Six Dragonflies

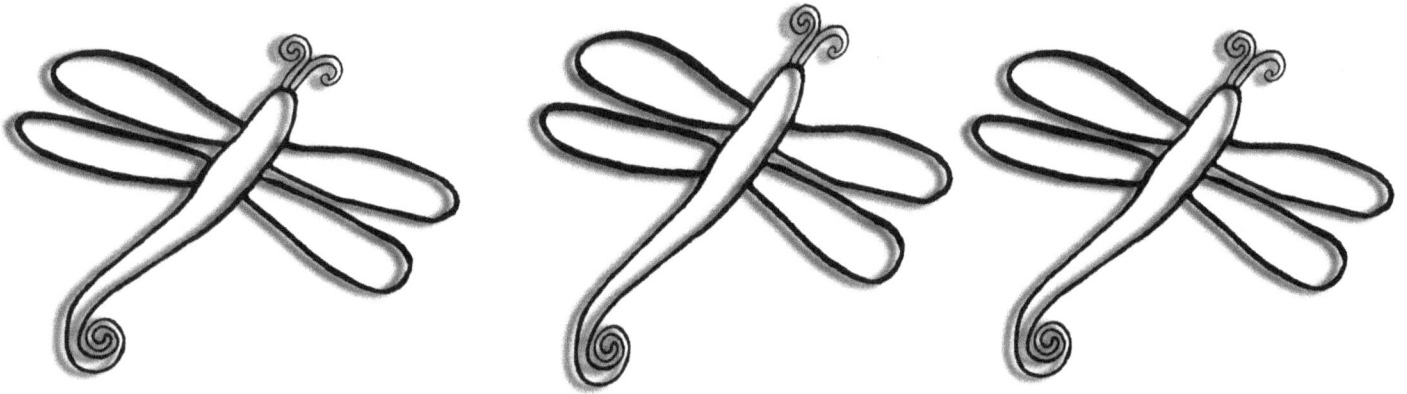

7

Seven Dragonflies

8

Eight Dragonflies

9

Nine Dragonflies

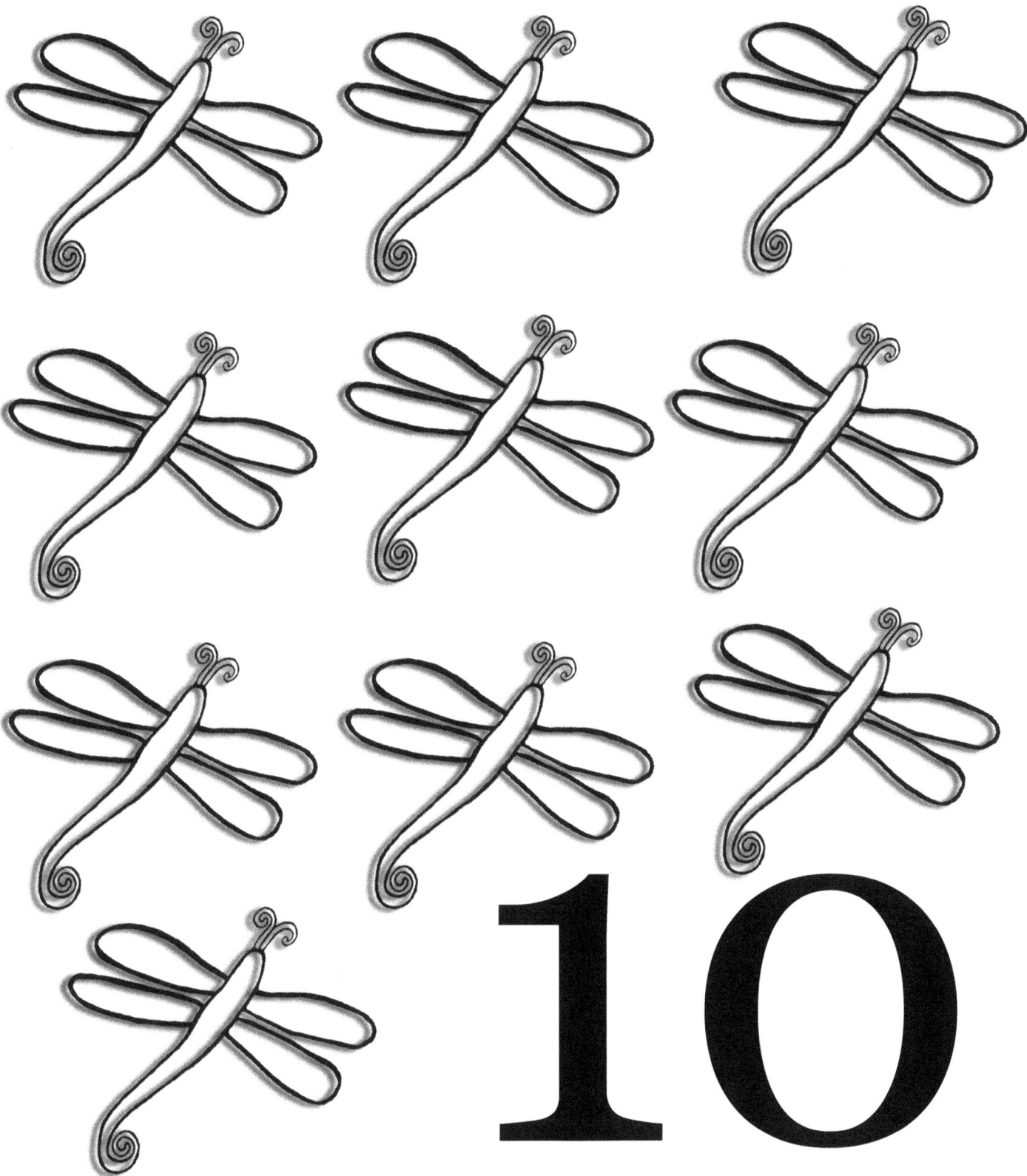

10
Ten Dragonflies

About Our Family

Brenda Sullivan lives in South Glastonbury, CT with her husband Paul and their daughter Katie.

They are avid nature lovers and gardeners who took their love of gardening to a new level by converting their 1.3 acres into a small farm called Thompson Street Farm LLC.

Brenda is an herbalist and market gardener who specializes in growing lavender, medicinal herbs and flowers. She also makes handcrafted goat's milk herbal soaps and herbal bath products using the herbs, flowers, fruits and vegetables grown on their farm or purchased from other local farmers.

More information on her bath and body products can be found at www.farmtobath.com

Katie, the love of their life and the center of their universe, has a number of serious medical conditions including severe cerebral palsy, epilepsy and very limited vision. She is nonverbal and wheelchair bound but these challenges have not prevented Katie from experiencing life.

Katie experiences the world on her terms with the help of assistive technology, other sensory, adaptations and years of homeschooling experience. Katie understands basic concepts and has developed many interests including an appreciation for music, painting with her Mother, and listening to stories.

She loves being outdoors and we've discovered that enabling her to experience the natural world has been Katie's best educator. This has been our inspiration for creating nature themed children's books.

Connect with Brenda online:
www.brendajsullivanbooks.com
www.thompsonstreetfarm.com
www.farmtobath.com
www.livingandlovinherbs.com
Facebook.com/brendajsullivanbooks
Facebook.com/livingandlovinherbspodcast

Other Books By Brenda J. Sullivan

Children's Books

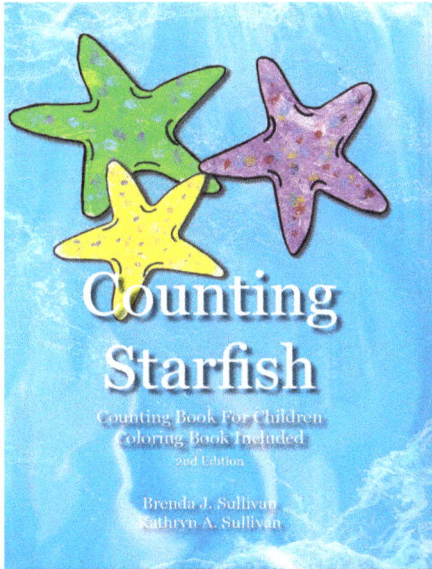

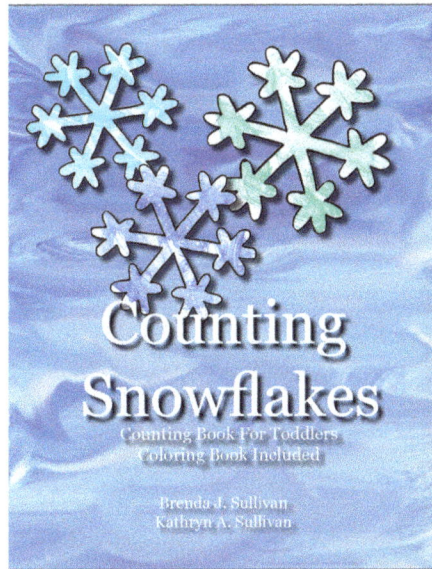

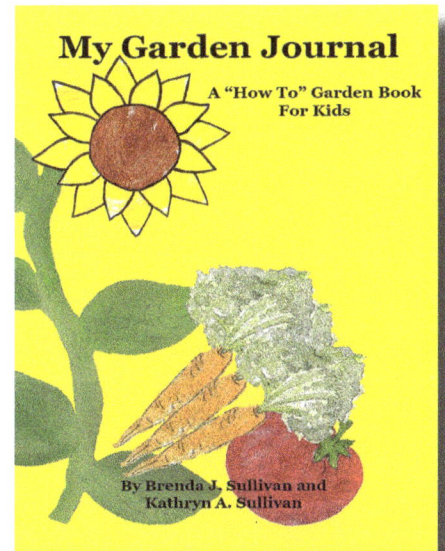

Counting Starfish
Counting Book For Children
Coloring Book Included
2nd Edition
Brenda J. Sullivan
Kathryn A. Sullivan

Counting Snowflakes
Counting Book For Toddlers
Coloring Book Included
Brenda J. Sullivan
Kathryn A. Sullivan

My Garden Journal
A "How To" Garden Book For Kids
By Brenda J. Sullivan and Kathryn A. Sullivan

Available in all stores and libraries - just ask!

Journals

Lavender Journal
Notebook

Lavender Journal
Notebook
Volume 2

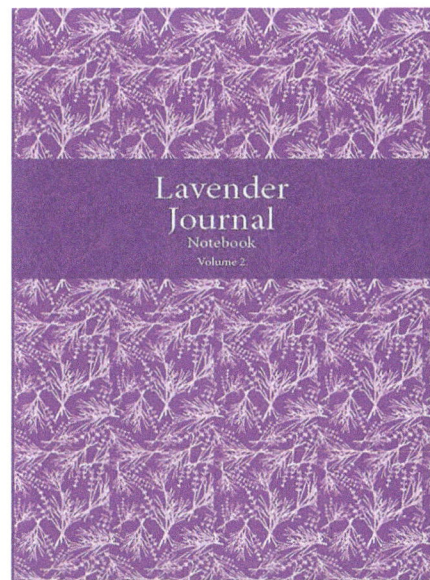

Available on Amazon

www.ingramcontent.com/pod-product-compliance
Lightning Source LLC
Chambersburg PA
CBHW042354030426
42336CB00029B/3483